INTRODUCTION

It's streetwise. It's intimate. It's postmodern. It's domestic. It's urban.

The fifth in Friendly Street's very successful New Poets series is a remarkable aggregation of talent. The three collections – selected from a formidable number of submitted manuscripts – represent the vanguard of South Australian poetry.

These first collections of poetry by Julian Zytnik, Ioana Petrescu and Maureen Vale are fresh, yet rich in experience and subtlety. Take the journey.

Stephen Lawrence
CONVENOR,
FRIENDLY STREET POETS

T0357926

FRIENDLY STREET

new poets
five

I Say...
IOANA PETRESCU

Twisting the Rainbow
MAUREEN VALE

The Love Within My Stare
JULIAN A. ZYTNIK

Friendly Street Poets

WAKEFIELD
PRESS

Friendly Street Poets Incorporated
in association with
Wakefield Press
Box 2266
Kent Town
South Australia 5071

First Published 1999

Book design and typesetting by Tabloid Pty Ltd, Adelaide
Printed and bound by Hyde Park Press, Adelaide

ISBN 1 86254 4476

Friendly Street is supported by the
South Australian Government through Arts SA.

ARTSA

CONTENTS

I SAY...
Ioana Petrescu

Ioana Petrescu is a Romanian university lecturer and poet,
currently a PhD student at The Flinders University of SA.
She started writing poetry in English when she came to Australia.
Ioana has performed regularly at the Friendly Street venues,
and has had poems published in Australia, New Zealand and
Romania, in newspapers, magazines and on the internet.

ACKNOWLEDGEMENTS

The Canberra Times, Overland Extra!,
Friendly Street Reader No. 21, Friendly Street Reader No. 22,
Deep South (New Zealand), *Famous Reporter, Poetrix, Redoubt,*
ABC – Radio National (*Poetica*), *Centoria*

For **Emil** and **Sergiu**,
my parents,
my friends,
and the Friendly Street audience

THE POEMS

Eyes like a mirror

Language is not my mirror.

In the morning I put on
some non-unproblematic
representational qualities
like being strong, being brave.
I add a dash of lipstick
to my smile
and – in haste –
I sip at the coffee I make bitter
to get used to the taste of the day.

Language is the prism I use
since Joyce made me throw away
"the cracked looking-glass of a servant".
I wish, I beg, I pray
to be contemporary
NOT contemptible
in my art –
which cracks at the slightest flicker
of eyes reflecting my eyes.

PART I

THE "HIGHBROW" THINGO

Definition

To Randall

What is post-modernism? –
an academic was asked.
The question caught him unawares –
he gasped and it took him a minute or two
to recover.
Post-modernism is a fatal word –
he answered.
Just like post-mortem and post-coital,
what it basically means
is that the fun is over.

In Bed with Philosophers

The student lies in her bed
next to Foucault's *History of Sexuality*
just like Alcibiades next to Socrates.
She's managed to control her drives so well
that even Plato would have been proud of her.

In fact she's fast asleep.

When she wakes up in the morning
she'll find in bed
the usual objects and traces of pleasure –
the book – crumpled at her feet,
and the quilt – stained by the marker pen.

For the next exam
she'll have to sleep with Derrida.

My Universities

I was about 20 and my *id*
developed a love-hate relationship
with Sigmund Freud.
My *superego* had a difficult time controlling the *id*
who was juggling with complexes.
My *ego* tried to mediate between the two
to no obvious effect.
By the time I graduated
I had realised the terrible truth:
I was doomed to see a woman
in each flower
and a man
in each snake.

Socratic Dialogue – 20th Century

Teacher, I'm confused, teach me of wisdom.
    The teacher does not answer.

Teacher, I feel emotion, teach me of love.
    The teacher keeps silent.

Teacher, I need to explain things, teach me the power of words.
    The teacher won't speak.

The sun goes down. Teacher and student
walk side by side. They share
the silence.

PART II

OLD-FASHIONED LOVE POEMS

Lost

I went to the beach
with a well-defined purpose:
to look attentively
through clear shallow water
and see if I could find
your shadow.

Question

If I look at you
what will you do
with my gaze?

Will you put it in your briefcase
next to unresolved paperwork,
or in one of your pockets
next to hankies and minties
so you can deal with it
later?

Letter

I wrote you a love letter
with a stick in the sand.
I dotted all my 'i's with shells
and used crab legs for commas.
Here and there I drew hieroglyphs
invented just for you
as I don't know the real ones.
You didn't answer my letter.
Could it be that you didn't get it?
It was there in the sand
for two days and two nights
before it was washed away by the tides –
first the shells,
then the crab legs.
The hieroglyphs faded away last
always pointing to the direction
where you could have found me.

PMT

She's got a headache.

She doesn't feel like making love
or having sex, for that matter,
although good sex
is recommended for headaches –
it apparently reduces the stress
of knowing that
ultimately
you're bound to be just yourself
by yourself.
Ghastly thought –
hence the headache.

Partners

I like my coffee black, hot
so that it burns my lips and my tongue.
But, since you have offered me some,
I'll accept it from your hands
as it is –
cold, white and sweet –
exceedingly sweet.

PART III

NEW WORLDS

Empathy

Shall I say this again
he asks because of my frowning
which means concentration to me
and lack of understanding to him.
I know that he thinks politically correct –
no, I'm not silly,
perhaps just a little bit handicapped
by accent, culture and hair colour.
Why is it that all fairies are fair-haired,
I'm thinking while he is telling me
the same thing
again and again
forming each word clearly
speaking slowly and omitting colloquialisms.
I'm lucky, think I,
last time I frowned
he used his eyes, mimicry and large gestures
to add content to words which seemed empty.
Birds with leaden wings, said Virginia Woolf,
think I, while he is saying the same thing yet another time.
I'll have to smile to end this conversation, I think,
a nice smile which means social convention to him
and joy, emotion or humour to me.
We are both tired and need a break,
we'll probably converse more
later, much later.

The Break

During the break he tells me
in his broken English
about his profession, house and family
that got suddenly lost in a war
somewhere in the Old Country.
He steps aside to let me go in first
while struggling to tell me
about nihilist philosophers.
He holds the chair for me to sit down
and orders coffee for both of us
asking discreetly what kind I prefer
and passing the information to the waitress
who stares in disbelief.
He sits at the other end of the table
talking about the Renaissance now
without demanding eye-contact
or conventional smiles.
When the coffee arrives
he takes no sugar or milk
and drinks it hot.
He draws the chair for me to help me stand up
and looks at his watch.
I go now, he says,
and I'm back in the here and now,
back from the Old Countries
where I spent the last twenty minutes.

Two Lousy Days

To Sergiu

Day 1

My son has to take slaters to school
for the science lesson.
I look up the word in the dictionary.
It says: "small crustaceous animals".
This doesn't enlighten me much.
My son shows me his fingernail:
"They are like this",
he tells me
full of hope,
but this doesn't make me any the wiser.
"The teacher told us they live in gardens
under leaves and rocks", he says.
We go to our minuscule backyard
behind the flat,
but you can't get a lot of leaves and rocks
for a few dollars a week
and slaters are definitely not included.
My son goes to sleep in tears.
I've been defeated by slaters.

Day 2

Next day I take my son to school
as usual.
He stands in the line head bent
no jar with slaters in hand.

A freckled little girl
comes right up to him,
ponytail bouncing.
"Show me your slaters",
she says,
"I'll show you mine."
My son blushes violently
and runs away.
I stand by helplessly.

I send a message to Europe:
"What the hell are slaters?"
The answer is simply disarming –
slaters are woodlice!
My family suffered for two days
because of woodlice!
I go down the gully
and capture an army of woodlice,
which I take to my son.
"It's all right, mum," he says,
"meet my new friend Louise,
she's already given me some."

Doing the Correspondence

First Correspondent

We've known each other for a while.
These letters fit my thoughts tightly –
carved, wrought, neatly cut ideas
in balanced proportion with some emotion
"so the mind shouldn't eat up the whole territory".

Second Correspondent

I'm embarrassed. I shouldn't be reading this
and she shouldn't be writing it.
The screen glares in my face
– and I feel nothing but pity –
religious, political, sexual convictions
in their bare obscenity
– and I feel nothing but pity.
I press 'trash'.

Third Correspondent

Hi. I've read Derrida and I've been to the market.
The first is a frustrated Marxist,
the second – a pleasure.
You know those gems, stones and beads –
I felt them. I didn't know I loved jade –
it's smooth and opaque
like Wittgenstein's theory.
It's rounded and fulfilling
like a Freudian thought –
yours truly.

These people feed (on?) my thoughts.
I'm tired now…and I love it.

Dear I,

His letters open like fridges –
there's an effort and then – pop! –
all of a sudden
the door opens
and the cold breathes in your face.
His letters read like fridges –
neatly arranged food…for thought.
And the door pulls at your hand
and before you know
it jerks shut
with a spasm.
Tightly, neatly shut,
like fridges.
And if you pull
it won't open again
for a while.

Best wishes.

My Lyric I

To Tom Shapcott

And now let me read for you
my Eastern European poems,
says the lecturing poet.
I changed my style and my voice
to write these – you know
another style, another way of positioning
the lyric I
towards the subject matter.
I listen carefully,
then go home and think –
what shall I be writing now?
I'm terrified by the fact
that I don't know what I'll be writing.
Is my lyric I lurking somewhere
in the dark abyss of my conscience
waiting for the moment when I sit down to write?
What if writing is not the only thing I do
in an Eastern European way?
What if I'm sitting, breathing and blinking
in an Eastern European way?
Even now, when I'm thinking of a new poem,
am I already positioning my lyric I
in a funny angle towards the subject matter?
Genius and/or difference,
say the editors,
will get you published.

Well, I don't know about genius,
but I surely have vast quantities of difference,
which, if allegations were true,
should keep me in print
forever.

A Question of Image

I know Dracula, believe me,
where I come from he is at home.
He turns up every night at 12 sharp
to oblige the tourists.
His long fangs do not shine in the moon rays
as bright as they used to,
you know, recession, no money
for fancy dental care products,
and blood quality decreasing every day...
He spends a lot of time polishing the sign
above he entrance –
"Transilvania" it says,
but tourists still think it's misspelt,
they prefer the version with double "s" and "y".
They wander all over the place aahing and oohing,
some take photographs, others shiver obligingly.
When they all leave, Dracula's birds make nests
out of Coke cans and fast-food wrappings.
"It's difficult to stay in business these days,"
says Dracula while refreshing his make-up.
"They've all read Bram Stoker's book.
They've all seen the movie;
I MUST MATCH THE IMAGE."

MIDDLE-OF-THE-ROAD POEM

***

When I want to get rid of my poems
I write them.
Much later,
when I feel as generous
as to forgive them
for disturbing me,
I read them.
Some of them
are like those mirrors
which grotesquely distort your image
at markets and fairs.
Sometimes,
if I read on
I might recognise myself
in some of them
and it's good,
because then
I, myself and my poems
can be friends again.

PART IV

TRIFLES

Public Services

To Telstra

Whenever he needs
to listen to Chopin
he calls TELSTRA.
Of course, he has to call
at different times
to get different bits
of the Polonaise.
He considered buying a CD
but if you calculate closely
you come up with an unnerving result:
for $25 (which is the price of the CD)
you can get 512.5 bits of the Polonaise
for only 40c a call.
If you try at the busiest times
you can wait in the queue up to 10 minutes.
Delightful!
Ten minutes of Chopin
poured directly into your ear.
May I help you?
asks a friendly voice all of a sudden.
Yes, he says, please,
any Bach, or Mozart?

Creative Process

Story #1:

Boy meets girl –
they fall in love,
they marry, have children
and live happily
ever after.
Publisher's reaction:
PASSÉ –
nobody will swallow this.

Story #2:

Partner meets partner –
they fall in love,
they do not marry
because they can't get a divorce.
Publisher's reaction:
TOO REAL –
nobody will want to know.

Story #3:

Green-eyed monster meets eerie girl
escaped from an underground lab
where an experiment went terribly wrong.
They fall in love
and figure out some kinky way
to have "S" "E" "X".
Publisher's reaction:
BINGO –
now we're in business.

Travelling Guide for Modern Women

If you visit England and Germany
shave your armpits –
only ill-mannered women don't.
If you visit France
don't shave your armpits –
it's sexy.
If you visit Italy
do as you please –
nobody cares.
If you visit Australia
shave your armpits again –
well-wishers strongly recommend it.
I don't know about the North Pole,
but I have an inkling
that, up there,
shaving armpits
is not a hot issue.

To my mother who was approached by a parent and was told approximately this:

Teacher, teacher,
please let my daughter pass.
I know she's not the brightest
in her class.
I gave this matter
all my thought
and if she passes
she will not
become a lawyer or physician,
computer scientist, accountant
or beautician –
nothing to bring her money, fame
or a secure future.
Oh, please, just let my daughter be
a teacher.

Modern Communication

The employee gives me a professional smile.
"Good morning! Can I help you?"
"Yes, please. I'd like…"
The phone rings.
"Excuse me."
She answers the phone.
She is very professional on the phone.
The conversation takes seven minutes.
"Now, you were saying…"
"Yes, please. I'd like…"
The phone rings.
"Excuse me."
She answers the phone.
She is very professional on the phone.
The conversation takes seven minutes.
"I'm so sorry. Now, you were saying…"
The phone rings.
I've got an idea.
I go to the phone booth next door
and I call the office.
She answers the phone.
No physical presence – no eye contact,
problem solved.
Communication proceeds.
Our conversation takes
about seven minutes.

Means of Communication

The office is not attended at the moment,
but if you leave a message,
your name and phone number,
we'll get back to you
as soon as we can.
He leaves the message
and then calls his mother.
I'm not in now,
please leave a message.
Hi mum, he says –
and suddenly feels like calling
his girlfriend.
Hello, if you hear this
then obviously
I'm not available now,
so, please leave a message.
Can I see you this weekend?
he shouts into the receiver.
When he comes back from work
in the evening
the machine gives him
three messages
saying basically the same:
"Sorry we couldn't reach you."

WINDING DOWN

Metaphysics

My senses are aroused by the purity of other presences.
My mind, still trapped in the fragrance of other attires,
replaces familiar images and noises with concentric circles
reverberating from the pebble I myself threw in the water.
I float from circle to circle. Unsplit rays sometimes shine
right from above.

Geometry

The sand is my writing space. I draw circles for birds,
rectangles for children and triangles for spouses. For me,
I just draw a line.

TWISTING THE RAINBOW

Maureen Vale

Maureen Vale grew up in Mildura. Graduated an English
teacher from Melbourne University, migrated to the gentleness
of Adelaide. Began trying to write at age four, and still is
working towards MA (Creative Writing) at Adelaide University.
Relaxes best browsing in libraries, bushwalking and with Tom,
her erudite Dachshund.

ACKNOWLEDGEMENTS

Iron Lace (University of Adelaide, 1998) for 'Wisdom of
the Plum' and 'Afternoon Tea', *Friendly Street Reader No. 17*
for 'Olive Picker, Golden Grove', 'Retreat', 'It Always Rains
on Anzac Day' and 'Changes', *Friendly Street Reader No. 18*
for 'Gifts', 'Sergei Krikalev Ponders Ten Months in Space'
and 'Ice Man', *International Women's Day* for 'Musicians',
Friendly Street Reader No. 19 for 'Genesis', *On Tap*, Gawler 1997
for 'Bitter Almonds', and *Friendly Street Reader No. 23* for
'Hovering at the Edge'.

For Marjorie and
in memory of Robert.

THE POEMS

The Wisdom of the Plum

One plum in March
mellowed to purple,
rich with summer.
Plump and voluptuous
this fruit a descendant
of Eden's sagacious tree.
Crisp and clean,
bright-skinned, white-fleshed
neatly seeded,
apples hold no mystique.
Nor the pomegranate
a bowl of gems
that shine unfleshed
cold on skin as rubies.
No-one loses her soul
in pomegranate abandonment.

Eve felt the plum, dented it a little
watched it hanging
indolent on a thin stem
sensuous as the coiled serpent
egging her on.
She squashed the fruit
with her artful tongue,
licked, swirled and squeezed
its amplitude through teeth and cheeks
splashed juice down her chin.
And learnt the pleasure
of sticky hands and face,
the messy blessing of over-ripe fruit

The tree's fecundity
was in her mind later
when she coupled with her man
in their sweaty cave.
As she stood before God,
wearing Plum trees
and blaming the snake,
she clutched Adam with one hand,
with the other a Plum stone
and rubbed its roughness
between finger and thumb.
She took it with her
when they left
A seed to plant in Earth's first winter
a memoir of Eden for her heirs.

Responses

We gaze, over coffee, through the window.
"What are the answers?" she asks.
"There are no answers," I say
"only birth, death
and a space to fill in between."
Noticing outside a lustrous Gum
whose leaves titter
at the slight breeze,
a dark bird
that pushes its way
into a thick white bush
busily nesting,
clumps of Impatiens
snuggled at the base of a Prunus
as she shakes her hair of new copper.
Four stringy lads on the grass
toss Orange peel tidbits of sun,
at one another
and gurgle in half-grown voices.

No answers but the season's cyclic urge
to begin again.

Figs

They stood, a steady row along the ditch,
their solid trunks and thick rough leaves
a sturdy defence aaaagainst ferocious elements.
My grandfather and the starlings
kept watch over hard green knobs
mellowing through autumn to ripeness.

He hated the birds that swarmed and squawked
made sorties upon ripening fruit.
Each day he checked and squeezed his figs
patrolled the ditches to shoot the marauders
and feed them to his cats.

The figs which obsessed him were never sold,
simply dried or churned into jam;
but that line of stocky trees holding the soil
were his campaign medals
which embodied all his battles
with rabbits, the Bank and weather.

Their foliage fluttered like proud flags
on behalf of all his orchard.
His triumph as to limp slowly, a worn warrior,
to a cool corner of the back room.
His black eyes gleamed, his old scarred fists
filled my little hands with fruit.
I clutched them in the dimness
felt their unpecked, unmarked perfection
accepted his trophy of war and love.

Olive Picker, Golden Grove

Woman smudged as history
muted skirt dipping low
between black scarf, black stockings.
She smacks at bushes with rods,
fluttering leaves
ancient, silver-tipped,
bringing down purpling fruit
onto stained cloths.
Battered olives fall
as centuries tumbling.
Her stand of trees
a blurred background
for bright gashed hills,
impertinent buildings,
planted vegetation –
cute yellow-green shrubs,
ash trees turning gold now
echoing the suburb's name…
along four lanes of new bitumen,
a landscape shrieking
today's place to be.
Still she swings her old sticks
turning one more crop
to steep in old jars
from times ingenuous
as olives in brine.

Gifts

My father sprayed tar on roads,
brought home scents of shimmering bitumen,
a breath of warm air at day's end
and red hands greasy with sweat.

I used to watch him work with clammy concrete
stirring stone and water in a well,
to pour carefully, trowel to and fro
until it was glassed perfectly
under loving fingers.
Later I caught the scrubbed tang
of hands washing away
fragments of his skill.

River mud came home with him
dragged on long boots after floods,
dense ooze darkening everything it touched.
He scraped its ugliness from him,
leaving heaps of foreign mire
on newspaper he twisted like a rabbit's neck, and burned.

Sometimes he took me to his workshop
to watch delicate sawdust flecks.
My nose drew sharp delight from pine and gum.
I saw his hands soften,
gently coax wood to change and grow
with his craftsman's secrets.

On Sunday afternoons, softer still
he sat priming his pipe
amidst the pungent smell of fallen tobacco
and uncorked whisky.
　　　This his bequest;
　　　conjuring hands, woven aromas.

Going Home

River gum's drooping bough
arches itself to a frame.
My camera solidifies
a familiar green parrot.

High water now.
The river fulfilled
holds toes of pelicans
skimming into plenty

And forty years on
fish of great lineage bustle,
grandchildren's grandchildren
of those we caught together,

My mother says he came to this bend, too
staring out his demons.
I never knew we cried our pain
to the same trees, watched by
the same possums' saucer eyes.

The cemetery is covered with lawn,
my father's grave has settled.
Gold letters on brown granite
need repainting.

And the trees have grown,
the crimson Ficifolia in flower.
My mother notes it.
He wanted to be buried under a Gum.

These snapshots, washed patiently by years
make perfect prints,
dazzle like sun on tin
water my eyes.

This place carries my myth,
a tortuous current
running through my blood.
A quart, they say, is enough.

I leave my father
to his plot by the river,
unable to rebirth our past.
And slip away on foreign number plates.

Sergei Krikalev Ponders
Ten Months in Space

In there, up there
it was too different.
Quiet, even with the crackling
radio communication.
Weightless, that ultimate floating
unlike anything they simulate.
A miniature world –
ship in a bottle,
garden in a jar.
Contained absolutely
having your own existence
spinning in your own orbit.
Of course my life changed
while I took time out.
But change is measured in seconds,
first grey hair
another speck of dust on a worn wall.
They kept it waiting for me, that's all,
their capsule of time
to exchange for mine.
When they took me from the cocoon I'd spun
they wanted me to be grateful.
I was thin, they said,
but they were grotesque
cowed by gravity, pulled out of shape.
It wasn't coming back to a different place.
Not returning.
Not a homecoming.
More like a terrible birth.

Ice Man

Rich brown gem
set in ice
strung on history.
Journeying further
than imagination
into a time trap
of technology
his being probed scientifically.
From cold and simple death
resurrected to colder
museum artifacts
filling large spaces
from his crevasse coffin.
Five thousand years
waiting to be found.
Longer than family's hope
for their hunter's return.

Musicians

Winter sun sneaks into the mall
dodging building shadows,
making small patches woven into circles
of drifting people.
Two music-makers squat, low and dark,
sending out quivering compelling sounds
of Didgeridoo and beating sticks,
trying to wriggle through dense structures
to endless sandhills under dazzling stars
where sounds call out forever on a frosty night

Where warriors in ochre and feathers
shuffle meaning into old stories,
raising dust and purpose.
But the trembling of the long tube
fades against shops and shoppers.
The clapping sticks stumble,
busking out of place, out of time.

Genesis

Your long ancestor
must have been beautiful too,
seducing new woman with apples.
Though he lost his legs for it
and she, humankind.
How he must have glowed in his sensual power,
twisting thickly round the new-spun legend tree.
Creation was his
as he poured loving words and muscled life
into her naked mind.
So both were damned, he to crawl
bellied forever to earth,
to carry loathing and fear.

He must have been lovely as you now,
lying in the sun
shining shoe-polish black,
head raised, bright-eyed,
your belly scarlet-tinged –
is that our blood?
You wait ready to slither
fast as light to the creek.

And evil is beautiful still.

Bunyip Chasm

Long and deep in the dreaming
this red gorge gauged
when bloated Akurru
dragged his great length
home to rest.
Now the river bed snakes
on smooth pebbles,
its chasm grips a wedge of blue
squeezed between cliffs.
There an eagle soars,
a dark boomerang,
wing tips link rock and sky.
Small creek sounds
tease out ancient stories
that linger waiting to be told,
and hide beneath shimmering sun
in tiny pools.
Rich silence holds in trust
water, rock and sky.
All of it bonded,
saved by myth by time
except for the yellow-eyed goat
balanced above the spring
and me.

Retreat

I have a first line
bold upon the page.

If only the wattle
wasn't shining,
shocking green parrots
whipping a corner of vision,
a small new bird
calling sharp as tin,
red gums twisting my mind
into old shapes
and the mountain misting
its summit secrets.
Bush perfumes infiltrate,
closing me in;
and an emu stalks me
refusing to believe
poems are inedible.

My first line looks insecure,
left when I deserted
to follow three wallabies
peeping from spiky shrubs
on the track up the bluff.

Wilpena Pound, June 1997

He peers and pokes, the young geologist,
searching out fossils to support his cause.
One thousand million years, he says,
this land writhed then, unsettled on its plates,
buckled and forced up the folded mountains
from their old sea bed.

His mate drums up excitement
with stirring tales of Man's adventuring.
He strokes the homestead's rough stone.
Settlers ran sheep, were beaten by drought.
John Hill planted wheat. 1890s.
With five sons, built a road
hammered iron spikes, chopped and hauled logs.
"Two years," the guide says, and halts.
"Two years! Ten years on, flood destroyed it
I want you just to stand, get the atmosphere.
Understand their hardships."

On this day, the pound is sleek with tourists
imbibing their rations of science.
And if there's time,
between climbing St. Mary's Peak,
(to the saddle at least),
and flying over in cheeky little planes,
they may fit in another yarn,
the Adnyamathanta Dreaming,

Of two giant snakes who crawled across the country,
gorged on the gathered tribe,
then, sated, died to form the ranges.
The visitors find the legend quite, absorbing.
Quaint, magical, a lovely fable.

But there's a better Fairy Story for us now,
while cameras click in tune
with the bulldozer's drone
carving an International Resort.
The hills will cringe beneath the clutter.
But your magic Visa card
will buy you all the myths you need.

Hampton Village Ruins, Near Burra, S.A.

Only a few stones emptied of voice
occasional chimneys bereft of colour.
Autumn breeze creeps amongst the ruins,
tries to winkle out sounds between the rocks,
fails to stir lilting Welsh songsters
whose melodies cut the clear evening air,
or children calling, running
through rose-jewelled Pepper trees,
pattering away the morning.

Today the visitors come, glance,
flee the desolation
that chronicles a lost clan,
in the inconsequence of ruins.
And the wind keeps encouraging,
fluttering an odd leave here and there,
but the rubble, immutable, clutches its memories.
In the centre a Sugar Gum hurls its life
towards the sky.
A single magpie thrusts out his chest
carries the hushed ghosts' tune.

Busker

Winter sun flecks
shoppers in the mall.
A busker breathes his flute.
Music falls, puffs of sound.
Set on cold brick
he defies the crowd's noise.
His jeans cling to legs,
slender metal pipes,
his fingers icy tentacles.

No one cares
if he plays or not.
People glance through him,
bustle on with their own lives,
brush his aside.
He remains invisible
to shoppers in the mall.

But his music whistles gently,
warms their minds later
as they hustle home
through a winter's evening
thin as a gaunt flute.

It Always Rains on Anzac Day

It always rains on Anzac Day
on the old men in old suits
shuffling through puddles in the street
soaking the ribbons
dulling the hard-won
of medals thumping gently
on chests beating faster.
It drizzles on the dawn
coming gingerly, confused
grey night to grey day,
making the sodden flag hang limp,
muffling the bugle's grey call.
It rains on the soldiers
stubbornly holding their rifles
cleans off last summer's dust
and pigeon dropping
from their steady stone faces,
brightens the flowers
below the carved names lit with gold.
gives the memories a good drink,
freshens up muddy trenches,
brings back flies on desert sands,
waters ancient friendships,
stirs ghosts to walk,
grows glory, pain
and long yarns in the Bar
for a long wet afternoon.

Afternoon Tea

The funeral is over,
her coffin clothed in earth.
I take the dusty track,
red sand filters through my sandalled toes
dawdling back to tea and cakes
in her familiar ssssitting-room.
Behind her cottage
her garden bakes in heat.

I remember how she coaxed
colours from the soil,
planted fruit and vines
bulbs for Spring
and daisies that slept at night.
I remember her hands
channelled with grime
shaking dirt from carrots and beet;
her old dried hands
that gathered, chopped and cooked
six days a week,
but scrubbed and cleaned,
offered from a white cloth,
embroidered with forget-me-nots,
dainty crackers with sliced tomato
and onion slivers;
moist orange cake, sultana fancies
to visitors who held fine English plates
and played her courtly ceremony
each Sunday, and forever

Today the house swirls
with floral women and shiny-suited men,
Unfamiliar sandwiches circle the room
foreign sponges follow.
I slip outside
to seek her in her own red earth,
but she has been swallowed up
like crumbs in a linen napkin.
I have to brush away
the grit between my toes,
behind my eyes.

Swimmers

Adolescents in the river
snug in the current
brown arms like wings
spatter drops of joy.
Hurled forward
giant butterflies shining
against summer.
Sun golds water
flickers on stiff old gums
that grouch silently and watch.
River and trees hold the boys
who, drunk with delight,
flip their shallow strength
above the muddy dungeons of roots.
The river and the trees keep their time
let laughter flutter. They form a frame of age
against the impertinence of childhood
slipping away on the stream.

Changes

Winter's probably a sonnet
working to a rich conclusion
but spring comes
like a Haiku,
quick gasps of colour,
almond blossom
on dark limbs, dark day,
bulbs ejecting perfume
rosella bright enough to mate
calling high on grey boughs
evenings opening their eyes
and newness all over.

Hypatia's Last Drive

Hypatia, a brilliant mathematician and neo-platonist
philosopher, taught an ascetic lifestyle. She was murdered by
Alexandrian Christians in March, 415 AD.

There's a scent of fear about the city.
My horses shake their heads, roll eyes, uneasy.
It's cooler now, too
I pull my sombre robe close,
shield me in philosophy.
Tonight I'm restless.
I feel mud spatter the wheels,
Difficult to keep my mind on purity.
I am tired.
Sometimes, alone at rest, I am disquiet
In the darkening evening, a pang,
a clutching at my breath.
Almost a wish, perhaps.
Strange how body fights for its due.
I have striven for Godliness –
how much the Gods only see –
to attain final, absolute power of thought,
that dazzling unfettered soul.

Only when I'm alone
face to face with myself,
I feel a little splinter in my head
digging with sharp pain
and yearn to feel
the jab of other pain
fingernails digging my excited flesh

To have run, stinging from rain;
and burned from sun and sweat on my bare neck.
Even to have been angered by children squabbling,
or to have found comfort from tiny hands.
I might have dressed to please,
looked in other eyes to see myself,
felt an unshaven cheek graze mine
that other life where blood is a torrent
where heart cries out, batters ribs.

These blasphemies shock: a lightning bolt.
Thunder of men, running on the street.
My horses lurch and stumble.
My mind shatters, jarring to futile shards.

Bitter Almonds

Almond blossom infant white
edges spring closer,
promises fruit neatly hugging limbs.
Nuts for steel-beaked crunching parrots
and me.
Here, though, birds come once
leave my tree to silence.
The flowers mock us,
nuts to come
like acid on the tongue,
eating away bland spring.
I should chop the sprawling tree,
leaving space for obedient plants
to carry the myth, the cornucopia.
Its grimness feeds me
a taunting season of unfulfilled pledges.
But the almond tree will stay
this year at least,
and I will watch the flowers
fall away like Confirmation vows.

August, Intensive Care, Glenside Hospital

Scent of prunus
wriggles into my nostrils,
pink petals fall.
I had not noticed Spring before
and I am not ready.
Winter coats me,
hangs on me easily with rain-soaked leaves.
From my bed I can see only concrete.
Locked doors and concrete.
Apart from a patch of grass
where young men with shaggy hair
tramp religiously on the hour
misted in cigarette smoke.

But Spring has come.
Inside, penned like chickens
we move to the beat of wind-played rain
into plastic chairs on a blue floor
which mimics sky.
We wander along a cream corridor
waiting. Afraid they'll come
to push us into Spring,
to open our overcoat minds
to a world of colours
where eyes live and heads sit high.

We want to stay in our coop,
ignore the world of sun.
We are paused timeless,
hide in corners
shuffle back and forth
between nothing and nothing.

As they open the door for me
I tremble out to Spring
holding the plastic bag of myself
under the scent of prunus.

Hovering at the Edge with Virginia.

Recurring bouts of madness plagued both her childhood and married life, and in March, 1941, Virginia Woolf took her own life.

Publisher's blurb, Virginia Woolf,
A Writer's Diary, 1978.

You can find no escape
from the storm that thunders
around your bare head,
and that black doubt
that squirms through brain cells
and blocks your mind
to make all things void.
Those confident moments of glory
become squashed leaves in mud.
Those words which flowed
are clichés sung in a foreign tongue.

You dread that aberration
when your mind stumbles on ice,
when you slip and skid
seeking your own bright space
where your sight is clear
and you know trees will bud
and drops of Spring dew hug fresh grass.

You fight to fill your day,
clean the kitchen, sweep the path.
Keep yourself busy
though your body aches for peace,
to retreat to your deep bed
block your ears
and hide in a cave of blankets,
a hibernating animal.
You let your thoughts straggle
along the foggy routes
of a bizarre landscape.

On the day you have no more to give,
you watch your imagination slop away
like dirty water from a washbowl.
The mist that skims the surface
of that embracing river clears.
Stones fill your pockets
gallant as thoughts,
bolder than words;
you wade towards vanishing point.

THE LOVE WITHIN MY STARE

Julian A. Zytnik

Julian Zytnik was born in 1973 and has lived most of his life in the Adelaide Hills, whose vivid seasonal beauty has greatly influenced his work. Also highly formative was his Seventh Day Adventist background – tightly bound in rules, yet idyllic – crashing hard against the turbulent freedom of secondary school and university. The Julian Zytnik of today observes the world with curiosity and (mostly) healthy scepticism "… but behind the bars of that cage still lies a naughty little boy." His interests include playing cricket, gardening, travelling, wine, and now photography.

ACKNOWLEDGEMENTS

The following poems, some in different form, have been
previously published or accepted for publication:

'Skenes Creek Road' published in *Hobo*, March 1999

'Flight' to be published in *Myriad*, 1998

'Mr Symes Addresses the Book Launch' published in
Literature and Aesthetics Vol. 8, October 1998

'Lila Leaves the Farm' published in *New England Review*,
Spring 1998

'Grace' published in *Spindrift No. 11*, February 1997

I am extremely grateful for the assistance of the
South Australian Youth Arts Board (SAYAB).
Most of the poems in this collection were conceived
or substantially reworked during the winter of 1998,
while writing full time under a $3,000 SAYAB grant.

THE POEMS

Rubedo

Travelling Notes, May 1997

I Take My Coat

RUBEDO

The rubedo is the third stage of human development,
the redness of life "…where one discovers passion".

Robert A. Johnson

Chocolate

I drop the tan manila file,
watch the flight of loose paper
spill onto the table
and surrender to a deep nothing
as I turn towards the last fingers of daylight
poking through the door
and start my walk to Stop F1.

Friday night's peak hour ride has begun.
The window lights of Gazman
Cool Change and Sole 2 Sole
flicker on. Piccinato the valuer's
staying back late – I can see him
through the roof-to-floor glass
pacing and chewing the end of his pen.

Flordian fashions, Heidelberg Bäckerei,
Pagoda Wine and Dine,
a dusk flood chain of neon dots
creeping up Glen Osmond Road
slowly, slowly
into mother's arms.

The passengers' faces are drawn
long by the dull of a week.
I am gutted of desire
but don't mind at all –
you learn to accept the emptiness,
develop a trademark wry smile
and like Sally Jessy confessionalists
give away delicious titbits
of your private (or medical) sublife
to girl-flashes.
           Tonight
two schoolgirls offer me chocolate –
thick, dark bars of "Honeycomb Malt" –
they have their proven way
of easing pain
(and oh those first teen pashes
flood back again!)
                  but then the snatch
"... youth service this Sunday"
cleanses their appeal
of dance floor *lurrve*.
Christ drops on me like a penny

but I still want to reach them.
I want to reach out to others,
sing and smile like these girls
driven by faith and divine love.

I have always loathed creed
but am starved of it,
need it like chocolate.

At home the TV is soft with sport
and the air outside is soft with rain.
Wes Montgomery and Fats Waller
honeydrip off the deep yellow walls

and trust, trust fills the room.
It fills me, soaks up my week.
I feel like a schoolgirl
who offers chocolate to strangers
and watches the rain
through the window of a bus
without the weight of a past.

Nuances

The colours of your walking
fly to me along direct
extrasensory lines.
I cannot grasp
the life that these nuances make
but like a child with toys
take each one piecemeal
and play purposeless games.

Lila Leaves the Farm

She'd told Micky the foreman
where to go, even said it was
no wonder his wife had left him
for another woman.

Lila giggled as she told us
this final scandal,
the whites of her eyes
bright neon globes
against pitch-black skin
and the fluoro-green beads in her hair
as she blended into the narrative
with thick West-Euro accent
all the lascivious background titbits:

how he'd sized her up at the bus station,
how he'd said she didn't let him know
on the phone she was black,
and how they'd got her packing in the shed
for the sake of a good perv.

Then she walked
down the orchard row
for the last time, head up,
scuffing the silver dew of dawn
off the grass with her brand new Nikes.

The local pickers cheered and
tipped their hats to her in gratitude,
savouring her as if she were their
affluent Anglo-Belgian hero
in a lost Steinbeck novel.

Good, Cool, Best

and all the straight-up **good** men
szhooom from 24 to 36 K a year
sprouting and feeding on the remains
of black culture the bums
and all the latest **cool** teen suicides
they used to kick into the toilet walls
for 'hardness' when prefects
at all the **best** good schools

Smoke Love

Bridgewater Inn, 24/7/97

"Let me tell you 'bout my baby –
she sure got it goin' on,"
the front man gargles,
coming on oh so Andrew Strong.

Tracy the girl from Women's Clothing
sways her slow motion
smoke love by the stage,
unwhirling the Coles Myer
residue of the day
into the guitarist's
loin-axe swing.

        The guitar swaggers back,
"Yeah babe, I love you too.
That's it – shake it all off!
Show me some *girl*!"

Steve from the servo
raises his glass to her and cheers.
Now depressed over cigarettes,
she can't resist when he offers her one.
Harmless enough, she thinks.
Besides, I've got to have one now!

So he provides, Rollins sinew
pushing through the tight navy T-shirt
with "Eureka" and the white Southern Cross
stamped firmly on its short sleeves.

The smoke is like fog,
only blue and electrified.
It reeks of *nite*.
Even the Keno and the dogs
are blurred cinematic.

He tells her she's a good dancer,
calls her "mate", I think.
The song reaches climax –
extended drum roll
over the deliciously clichéd
descending blues-scale solo.

Eureka-man yells "Oh yeah!" then turns
to buy a beer for the ColesMyer girl
who's already sizing up the safety
of an exit by the side door.

Sign

Under the dim orange street light
I can just see a sign
in the window of The Professionals
Real Estate regional office:

"A free trip to Penang" –
just call one of the agents
for your land transaction needs
and you could be flung

into the destiny and rubedo of the glistening
coconut-oiled Mastrioanni by the pool.
You indeed could be his wide-eyed
expatriate apprentice-buddy, drink

cocktails with his wife and associates
under the thatched shelters and vivid palms
in air just as balmy and simple as this
identikit picture of life suggests.

No it's not all a trick, you know.
It's a genuine technique
for warding off reality and depression.
It's a mode of existence in its own right –

You take a trade wind,
thicken it sleepy with sea-vapour
(oppressive, but you'll love it in time
like a vindaloo masochist)

add a beach ball, a peeling boat,
a hung-up sandy wetsuit and some reeds,
then trim this postcard down
rectangular-flat –
                  and you've got your life
your *raison d'être* – a taut thin film
of Gatsbyan schtick-mystique
devoid of the grief of history,
a sliver of moon that casts no shadow.

Maya

Serving the Goddess Maya…costs one all reality
Robert A. Johnson

One day I want to
get you alone and ask you –
have you ever swum in the sea
during an Indian Summer
or driven to an old railway station
and watched children
being greeted by their mothers
while you yourself meet only
your own shadow of ridicule
and drown in a sea of tears

then if not for malingering shame
be filled with sudden love.

TRAVELLING NOTES
May 1997

To live in one land, is captivitie,
To runne all countries, a wild roguery
John Donne, '3rd Elegie'

Kalangadoo Country

near Mt Gambier, 10/5

The patchwork of plough-marked plots
dairy pastures and thicket
in the valleys below Kalangadoo
show an algid West-Irish dankness.

Cows graze by tall, skeletal copses
and their thorned underbrush;
kids back from school
take the dog for a walk, hoping
the drizzle will stay away before dusk

and Grandma's house
on the fringe of The Mount,
ineluctable after fifty years,
waits for the yearly pilgrimage
of her children
borne in roof-racked station wagons.

Moss thickens on the white
peeling paint of its walls
and rust creeps over
the wire sign that reads
'Lornmyr'.

Skenes Creek Road

Otway Ranges, 10/5

as we snake along
this wire-drawn thread of road
the car wheels flick up
terracotta pebbles and
bits of thick matt puddle-paste
onto the luminescent green

from the top of the ridge
the sea below
beats rock into a
jigsaw of caverns and bluffs
Aeolus the sea-wind
thrashing rows of *pinus radiatae*
as if slaves

the sheltered calm in its wake
holds silence
crystal droplets and creek reeds
delicate

the layered canopies of rare ferns
recall my own
organic stages of growth
my opacity just like
the mottled lichen and
the soft fog

The Gorse and the Briar

near Geelong, 10/5

the land of gorse and briar
pushes down from the ranges
in tentacle lines of scrub guarding the roads
and carries its clay-people
into a vast engulfing even

UK Girl by the Mock Fire

Melbourne, 12/5

A tanned, plump UK girl
with ruffled blonde morninghair
and a look of replete 'Oh yeah!'
after last night's sweaty
backpacker rendezvous

flicks over to the next page
of *Sex, Death, Enlightenment*
and sucks her middle finger like a dummy,
hand-sewn purple-striped pants
shifting and slithering
in front of the mock mallee-root fire.

Close Confines

Byron Bay, 20/5

The close confines of our companionship
drive me to a level of banality
I never thought possible.

I dwell upon the lamp-lights,
the wall-paint, the coffee prices here,
moving from the specific to the general
as if some revered academic,
drawing the vivid reds and greens
off the street like a sink drain
into a still, grey point

I even add a nasal inflexion
of Our Father to my voice,
aiming not to enlighten
but to buttress my dialectic power:
words compound authority,
authority confirms words,
and so on.

Flight

Byron Bay, 25/5

Salt-fat winds
whip and roll the late-autumn swell and
set the ethical timbre:
indulgence, excess
writhing free of habit's dull tug
into rip tide nites.

Boom baby
Booker-T-black throb
sets the meter:
a lilt and swagger of
flash-striped cotton pants
flared out and wandered by legs in
loose V motions.

Highway 1
serpentines out of town and
sets the path of flight:
an adrenaline ascent
through ranges wrapped in strangler figs
and fog
trailed closely
by a long, black, finned shadow
that screeches around greasy corners blind
trying to get at you and
bring you to judgment
but never will
and I am now
one like all here – a shadowed reinvention
who only knows himself
when incomplete.

Old Friend

Brisbane, 27/5

Here under the frangipani tree
with you at last
I want to display my new plumage
of beach and Memphis tones

eager to show my pace of change
from taciturn Julian Sands
to impressionable Brian Wilson,
sunlight sparkling in the frayed
rim of my fringe,
'60s AM radio hits
honeyed in my voice.
                              You, too,
want to distance yourself
from the libraries and the lattés –

all those letters to me
about cane toads, the house on stilts
and the air corrupt with humidity

had teased me like you were about
to burn me off at the lights
in a hot rod (on the way
to that surfing safari
you'd always mentioned).

And so now we show off our colours,
try to burn each other off at the lights,
see who can forget our pasts first.

You win.
Our featherings are respective
rather than akin.

Here under the frangipani tree
with you at last,
enduring existential singularity
cleaves us.

I TAKE MY COAT

Last Evening Run on the 165 Line

Punk kids in psychedelic vinyl
beat off boredom on tin cans
and surf word games
along frothing waves
of reefer-driven sniggering –

uncontrollable, cackling and croaking
like frogs, like kookaburras.

The patter of "pigs"   "shit!"
                "parents" "freak-out"
                "ouch!"
jolts us around to stare –

can you see
through the blanket haze
the love within my stare?

My white mask was shaped
under Eliot's instructions
then daubed in the clean pastel shades
of a Hopper afternoon

but a naughty little kid
still clambers on the underside
spraying Basquiat graffiti.
You'd know him –
his words buck and sizzle
just like yours.
Can you hear his same
kookaburra cackle?

Midnight in Late Spring

The dappled
lamplight in the trees
is naked as innocence
but pregnant with mysteries.

Pink candy-fluff flowers
push into the hot night
like new poetry –
quivering, baby-tender, pliant.

Spots of rain begin to puff
dust off the pavement
and a rattling swell of crickets
surges up from the empty creek.

Mr Symes Addresses the Book Launch

He approaches the stage
with a hint of swaggering dance,
head bent low
and cowboyesque,
self-satisfaction sweltering into a halo,
seasoned wood-carved game show smile
ready to meet the imminent applause.

The welcome is warm
but sharper than sanguine –
It has the bite of hunger in it,
a craving power that cuts and
shapes one's image no matter
what is said or done.

But the man in the Hawaiian shirt
is measured and cool
armed with a few ice-breaking jokes
and the eternal in-house critic,
a kind of paranoid literary Columbo
who shuffles suspiciously
across his mindscape and taps
a cigar on his cranium
every time he threatens a wrong move.

4:50pm, Friday Afternoon

A jaded professionalism
drags out the time
like a tired dog.

Ties slip loose, shoes
scuffle instead of clop;
restless eyes sneak wider,
envisioning cover bands
at seaside pubs
and boats moored
in island-studded inlets
near the Murray mouth.

They wait, walk and wait
and we watch them
through the coffee-shop window,
talking up the office minutiae
of our week,
picking shards of heroism
out of hours fading fast
in the smog of ragged lethargy.

The Room is Filled

The room is filled
with the unsolicited laughter
of front-bar backwash silt
sitting near the open fireplace.

Girls swing and sway on tables
clicking fingers to a boozy song
while others commune in
vanity and small addictions
all chasing the chimera
at the eye of the music
and in themselves
like Blue Devil jazz-cats
hunting each other in jam-whirls.

     and the *laughter*,
again the chittery laughter cascading…

Minor Court Testimony

This man in trim spectacles
and dandruff-dusty jacket,
hair spiked along the part
like a car salesman,
knows too well not to let sincerity
curdle hard pursuit of The Game.

He curls in his lips out of habit
(or purses them until bloodless)
pauses and strategically demurs;
he'll wait for one of the virgin Semaks
to burst into callow, canine entreaty
(then it will be easy).

Eyes in their deathbed sockets
glimmering but nearly cold
tell me with cop-hardened
Zen-mastery
          "Not at all,
it's business, just business."

Grace

Alcohol is the most artful of poisons.
It softens the heart and blood into a syrup
anaesthetised from hatred and torment.

It seduces us into childhood again,
that state with no unrequited questions
and no need to make distinctions,

where we break into madmen's waltzes,
supple, innocent and ecstatic –
Oh how you detest us, proud Gracie,

as you sip your coffee carefully
and peer through sharp blue eyes
at us, the alcohol-souls.

We froth like the head of a Guinness;
we were always too loosely defined
for you to play your shrill staccato upon us.

You prefer those sculpted
by principle and aesthetics,
hard-boiled in the long black's thick sediment.

Farewell to a Colleague

As we tie up these final matters
my pulse leaps and tingles
and 'colleague' blurs into *compagnero*.

I take today's headlines
and try to cast new bonds between us;
sadness the love-starved terrier

bites and nips at heel
as you give your spiel
on bad clients and Friday nite Scotch –

already I can feel
a warm malt ghost that intermingles
with gulped regrets deep in the throat,

      – then I take my coat.